CARING
• YOUR PET •

RABBITS AND GUINEA PIGS

Don Harper

AN INTERPET BOOK

© 1996 Interpet Ltd.,
Vincent Lane,
Dorking, Surrey
RH43YX

ISBN 1-902389-82-4

CREDITS
Editor: Helen Stone Design by: DW Design, London
Colour Separation by: Pixel Tech, Singapore
Filmset by: SX Composing Ltd., Essex
Printed in Slovenia by DELO tiskarna
by arrangement with Korotan Ljubljana

PICTURE CREDITS
Artists
Copyright of the artwork illustrations on the pages following the artists' names in property of Interpet Ltd.

Paul Davies: 28, 35, 39, 46   Wayne Ford: 6, 22, 26, 31, 38
Guy Troughton: 21

Photographs
The publishers wish to thank the following photographers and agencies who have supplied photographs for this book. The photographs are copyright of the photographer and have been credited by page number and position on the page: (B) bottom or (T) top.

Marc Henrie: 9, 13(B), 15, 16, 17, 23, 34, 40, 43, 45(B), 48(B), 51(T), 52, 54, 55
Cyril Laubscher: 4, 8, 10, 11, 12, 13(T), 14, 27, 32, 47, 48(T), 53, 57, 61(B), 63
RSPCA Photolibrary. S Burman; 19(B), E A Janes; 49, Judyth Platt; 5, 24, 41, 51(B), Colin Seddon; 20
David Sands: title, 19(T), 30, 37, 42, 45(T), 61(T)
Jacket photograph © E A Janes, supplied by RSPCA Photolibrary

Contents

Introduction

Rabbits and guinea pigs as pets

Few pets are easier to care for than rabbits or guinea pigs as these small mammals can be kept either indoors or in an outside hutch. With regular handling, they soon become tame and easy to handle and will not normally bite.

● **Above:** *Regular handling of your pet will make it tame and help to build a strong bond between the two of you.*

Daily care

Even so, it is important to think carefully before taking on pets of this type. You must be prepared to feed them and provide fresh water every day throughout their lives, which may be 15 years or more. Your pet will also need grooming and you will have the additional responsibility of cleaning out the hutch on a regular basis.

Constant companions

Both rabbits and guinea pigs live in colonies in the
wild and if you are keeping a lone animal, you will
need to give it plenty of additional love and
attention. Rabbits and guinea pigs can be housed
together in a large enough hutch, but in this case you
should choose one of the smaller breeds of rabbit, so
there is less risk of your guinea pig being trodden on
and injured by the weight of its companion.

Housing together

When keeping groups of rabbits and guinea pigs
together, it is important to ensure that there is no
fighting or unwanted young. Male animals are most
likely to fight if housed together and so it is best to
start out with two females if you are not intending to
breed them.

● **Above:** *Both rabbits and guinea pigs have lively
characters and make charming pets. They are both sociable
animals and so it is better to keep several rather than one on
its own.*

Rabbits and guinea pigs in the wild

Where do rabbits come from?

Although they originally come from Spain and nearby parts of the Mediterranean, today wild rabbits can be found all over the world. Throughout the centuries, rabbits have been transported to other continents where they have settled and bred easily and, in some places such as Australia, their numbers have grown to enormous proportions.

Rabbit-spotting

If you are out in the country you may see signs of wild rabbits and, if you are lucky, you may even

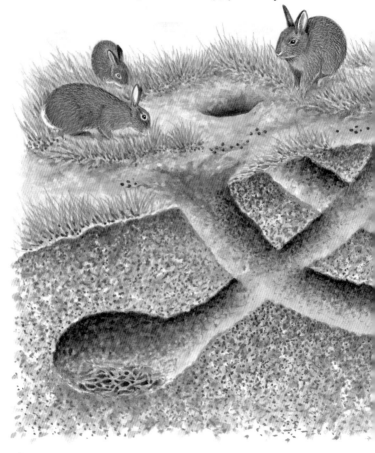

catch a glimpse of a rabbit itself. Early mornings and evenings during the summer months are good times for rabbit-spotting as the rabbits you see will probably be youngsters. At this age they are less likely to run to the safety of their burrows.

Rabbit burrows

The entrance to a rabbit's burrow will be quite obvious as the grass around it is likely to appear trampled and you will see rabbit droppings on scrapes in the earth nearby. Below the ground lies a network of tunnels and chambers called the warren where the rabbit sleeps and raises its young.

Where do guinea pigs come from?

Wild guinea pigs are found in northern South America where they live high in the Andean mountains. They do not burrow like rabbits but depend on finding shelter amongst the rocks and grasses. Like rabbits, they are a popular source of food for local people which is how they came to be domesticated.

● *Left: In the wild, rabbits are sociable creatures which live in colonies. Their society is focused around a shared warren which has a network of underground burrows linked to a series of hollowed-out chambers.*

The domesticated rabbit

Rabbits have been kept for food and fur in Europe for over 1,000 years and during this time they have been bred in many different sizes and colours. By the end of the last century, there were two main types of rabbit which were known as 'fur' and 'fancy'. Fur breeds were large and kept both for their meat and fur. Fancy rabbits tended to be smaller and were valued more for their appearance as they often had attractive markings.

● **Above:** *The British Giant White is one of the older breeds of rabbit which would have been kept for its meat and fur in the past. Today they are kept as pets, but can grow to be quite large and heavy and so can be difficult to handle.*

Pet rabbits

During this century, rabbit breeding has led to the development of more breeds and there are now over 100 to choose from. Sadly, some of the older breeds have become less popular and are now quite rare, but attempts are being made to prevent these more unusual rabbits from becoming extinct.

The domesticated guinea pig

Guinea pigs have been farmed for food and fur in their native South America for over 2,500 years but they were not known in Europe until after the Spanish invaded South America in the early 1500s. The Dutch brought guinea pigs back from Surinam on the northern coast of South America in 1667 and they proved to be popular pets, becoming common all over Europe.

How they were named

No-one is sure how these rodents got their unusual name. It may have been because they came from Dutch Guiana, as Surinam was then called, or sold for the price of a guinea in the early days. Their body shape and grunting noises were probably responsible for their becoming known as 'pigs'.

● **Above:** *This guinea pig may not look much like a pig, but it is probably the squealing and grunting noises these creatures make which earned them their unusual name. Guinea pigs are also known as cavies.*

Choosing the right breed of rabbit

There are now over 100 different breeds of rabbit and, if you are interested in seeing a wide range, a visit to a local rabbit show will give you a clear idea of the size and appearance of many of the breeds. One of the most important things to consider when choosing a young rabbit is how large it will be when fully grown.

Choosing the right size
Smaller rabbits such as the Dwarf Lops or the Dutch are often the best choice as a pet. Their small size makes them easy to handle, whereas the larger breeds such as the British Giant or Californian are much heavier.

Dutch rabbit
In spite of its name, this breed was developed in Britain in the late 1800s and it has very attractive markings. The front part of the body, including the

legs and feet, are white and there is a prominent V-shape of white fur on the face. Dutch rabbits are traditionally black and white but they are also available in other colours such as yellow, chocolate and grey with white.

Netherland Dwarf

Netherland Dwarf rabbits were bred from crosses between Dutch and Polish rabbits and have soft, dense fur. They are fairly small, weighing just 1kg (2^{1}/4lb) and have short ears which are no longer than 5cm (2in). There is a wide choice of colours, ranging from pure white with red eyes to patterned varieties. It is particularly important to check the teeth of these rabbits as Netherland Dwarf rabbits are particularly prone to dental problems. In some cases, the teeth do not fit together properly which makes eating difficult.

● *Opposite:* The Dutch Tricolour rabbit makes an attractive pet which is small and easy to handle.

● *Left:* The Polish is a smaller and lighter rabbit than the Dutch.

● *Above:* The Netherland Dwarf is a cross between the Dutch and the Polish rabbit.

Lops

One of the most distinctive types of rabbit is the Lop, which has large ears that hang down permanently. Other breeds of rabbit only keep their ears down when they are resting. Lops have been bred for nearly 200 years and the oldest of these breeds is the English Lop. This large rabbit has wide, trailing ears which can be over 60cm (24in) long.

Dwarf Lops

Dwarf Lops are smaller than the standard Lop, weighing just over 2kg (5lb). They have shorter ears and make better pets than the English Lop as they need no special care and are friendly by nature.

Cashmere Dwarf Lops

The Cashmere Dwarf Lop is a cuddly-looking rabbit with longer, softer hair than similar breeds. The coat needs regular grooming to prevent it from becoming matted.

● *Left: The Cashmere Dwarf Lop was bred in part from the ordinary Dwarf Lop (above) and the Angora (top right).*

Angora

The Angora is one of the oldest of all rabbit breeds and has been kept for centuries for its wool which can be woven into clothing. However, Angoras are very demanding to keep because of their long coats and they need special housing and grooming.

Belgian Hare

Although it is confusingly called a hare, the attractive Belgian Hare is in fact a rabbit! It was given its name because of its slim shape and tall build. These medium-sized rabbits can weigh up to 4kg (9lb).

● *Left: The tall Belgian Hare needs to be kept in a suitably tall hutch.*

Rex

Rex rabbits were first bred in France in 1919 and have a soft, velvety coat. Their fur is soft because it has none of the coarser guard hairs usually found in a rabbit's coat. These rabbits also have short, curly whiskers. Rex rabbits do need some special care and you will need to provide a good layer of bedding as the fur on their lower legs can wear thin on a hard floor.

Among the most popular colours are Chocolate and Orange Rexes. A young Rex rabbit may seem to have a coarse coat as there are usually some guard hairs at this age, but these will be shed and not replaced as the rabbit grows older.

Black and Tan

Smaller and less common is the Black and Tan breed of rabbit which was bred by chance from wild and Dutch rabbits. Weighing just 2kg ($4^1/2$lb), it has soft, sleek fur. Other colours combined with tan, such as lilac or chocolate, are also available. These are known under separate names such as the Lilac and Tan.

● *Above:* The Black and Tan is smaller and rarer than the Rex (top).

Choosing a guinea pig

As with rabbits, guinea pigs have been bred in many different colours and patterns. There are different coat textures ranging from the Rex to long-haired Peruvians. Sleek, smooth-coated guinea pigs are the most popular as these are easy to care for and need little grooming. You may prefer a so-called 'self' variety which has a coat of all one colour, or there are Dutch guinea pigs with white areas in a similar pattern to rabbits of the same name. The range of pure colours is wide, from shades of cream and golden through red to chocolate and black.

● **Above:** *Guinea pigs may have patterned coats or may be 'self' coloured (below).*

● *Above:* The Abyssinian guinea pig has an unusual coat marked by ridges and rosettes. This strange hair growth is natural and doesn't need grooming.

Patterning

Smooth-coated varieties of guinea pig include the Agoutis which have light and dark bands on their individual hairs, creating a mottled appearance. Alternatively, the Tortoiseshell and White represents a colourful combination with bold areas of red, black and white giving these guinea pigs a unique patterning. There are also Himalayans, with black or chocolate noses, ears and feet offset against a pure white coat. These have red eyes.

● *Right:* Agouti guinea pigs are available in many different colours. From left to right: silver, gold and lemon.

16

Coat types

Abyssinian guinea pigs have ridges and rosettes which are formed by tufts of rough hair in their coat. Brindle Abyssinians which have red and black coats are especially popular. Their fur does not require a lot of grooming unlike Peruvian guinea pigs whose coats trail down along the ground.

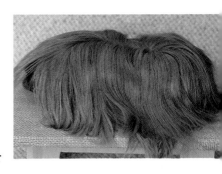

● *Above: Sheltie guinea pigs are better kept as show animals rather than pets as they require a lot of grooming.*

Long haired

Long-haired guinea pigs such as the Peruvian and the Sheltie are best avoided unless you are prepared to spend time each day grooming your guinea pig.

Newer varieties

New varieties such as the popular Rex with its cuddly appearance are still being developed. There are also Satins and Dalmatians which have dark spots like those of the famous dog *(pictured top on page 15)*.

17

Questions *and* Answers

I am thinking of getting both a rabbit and a guinea pig. What is the ideal age to introduce either of these pets to a new home?

Start with young animals as these will soon grow used to you and, with regular handling, they will become very tame. Rabbits will be feeding themselves by seven weeks old, whereas guinea pigs will be able to go to a new home when they are just five weeks old.

How can I recognise healthy animals?

Both guinea pigs and rabbits have lively, alert natures and a healthy animal should not sit huddled up with its eyes closed.

Check inside the mouth. The incisor teeth at the front should fit together·snugly. Unlike our teeth, the incisors of rabbits and guinea pigs continue to grow throughout their lives and are worn down as they gnaw their food. If the incisors in the top and bottom jaws do not meet properly, the animal will find it difficult to eat and the teeth will grow at a strange angle. This condition is called *dental malocclusion* and the teeth will have to be cut back at regular intervals throughout the animal's life. This trait is inherited so affected animals should not be used for breeding.

Check inside the rabbit's ears for signs of scabs caused by ear mites and the guinea pig's skin for any signs of severe dandruff or baldness, which may be caused by skin mites. Check that its bottom is clean with no staining or matted fur. The eyes and nose should be clean and clear and the claws should not be overgrown.

● *Above:* When choosing a new guinea pig or rabbit, it is important to check the teeth. Poorly formed teeth will need to be cut back regularly to enable your pet to eat properly.

● *Above:* Rabbit kittens are adorable when young, but you must be sure that a young rabbit can feed itself properly before it is removed from its mother to be your pet. A badly weaned rabbit will be weak and is likely to fall ill.

Choosing the gender

If you are simply seeking a rabbit or guinea pig as a pet, then the animal's gender will probably not be of great importance. It is sometimes said that does (female rabbits) are gentler than bucks (males), but this is not always the case.

● **Above:** *It is important to know the sex of any rabbits or guinea pigs you plan to house together. Males and females housed together may result in offspring you cannot care for.*

Breeding

It is important to know the sex of your pets if you are housing them in groups to avoid fighting or unwanted young. It will also be important if you are planning to breed them. In this case, it is usually better to keep more females and arrange for these to be mated with other people's males, as you will then have the resulting babies to choose from. A pair of females will make happy companions.

Sexing rabbits

It is not always easy to sex young rabbits, but once they are mature at five months old the difference will be more obvious. The gap between the two openings on the underside of the body close to the tail is shorter in does compared with bucks and, by this stage, the scrotal swellings in a male will also be obvious. You should avoid keeping bucks together in a hutch as they are likely to fight and can seriously injure each other with their sharp claws.

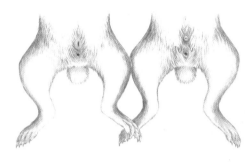

● *Above: In a female rabbit (left) the gap between the two openings near the tail is shorter than in the male (right).*

Sexing guinea pigs

To sex a guinea pig you will need to place your thumb and finger either side of the front opening. In the case of a boar, the male organ will appear whereas this does not occur with sows. Boars can be kept together, but avoid introducing one boar in to the cage of another as this is especially likely to result in fighting.

● *Above: The female guinea pig (left) has a smaller opening than the male boar (right). Gentle pressure applied to the sides of the opening will reveal the male organ in a boar. A vet will be able to confirm your pet's sex for you.*

21

Understanding your rabbit

Although previously both rabbits and guinea pigs were thought to be rodents, today only guinea pigs fall into this category whereas rabbits and hares are known as *lagomorphs*.

The teeth
The difference lies in their teeth. Rodents have two sharp incisor teeth in both their top and bottom jaws, whereas rabbits have four. You will be able to see the small second pair behind the large incisors at the front of the mouth.

The mouth
Behind these teeth, there is a gap called the *diastema* which allows the animal to pull in its cheeks as it eats to stop twigs and other tough material going into its mouth. At the back of the mouth there are molar teeth which are used to grind up the food before it is swallowed.

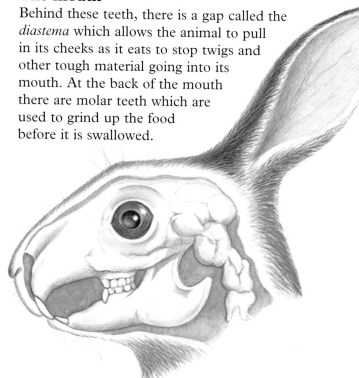

● *Above:* A rabbit's front incisor teeth are used for tearing plant food whereas the back molars are used for grinding.

● ***Above:*** *Rabbits suck in their cheeks when they eat to stop any sharp or tough material going into their mouths.*

Digestive system

Food passes down into the stomach and along the small intestine until it reaches a large, closed sac called the *caecum* where the tough cellulose in plants and vegetables is broken down by helpful bacteria. It is important to avoid sudden changes to your rabbit's diet as the bacteria need time to adapt.

Absorbing nutrients

Unfortunately, this part of the digestive tract does not allow the nutrients in the food to be absorbed into the body. Instead, the partially digested food passes out of the body in the form of soft *caecal pellets*. You are unlikely to see the caecal pellets because these are usually produced at night. The rabbit eats the pellets and this time, the nutrients are absorbed as they pass from the stomach to the small intestine. The rabbit then produces its typical large round droppings.

Understanding your guinea pig

Guinea pigs have a similar digestive system to rabbits and both are vegetarian. Unlike most mammals, guinea pigs cannot make Vitamin C and so it is important that your pet is fed a Vitamin C-rich diet every day. This vitamin is necessary for a healthy skin and without it, guinea pigs develop skin problems such as *scurvy*. The skin can crack and bleed in severe cases.

● **Below:** *A well-balanced diet comprising of seeds, nuts, cereals and plenty of fresh fruits and vegetables is necessary to keep your guinea pig's coat in good condition.*

CHECKLIST - Foods rich in Vitamin C

- Broccoli
- Dark green leafy vegetables
- Carrots
- Swede

Added Vitamin C

If you are keeping a rabbit and guinea pig together, it is important to ensure that your guinea pig is getting enough Vitamin C in its diet. You can give your pet tablets, but most guinea pig foods now have extra vitamin C added. Because Vitamin C is easily destroyed by the atmosphere, it is best to buy food in small amounts to ensure that it is always nutritious.

Keeping claws in check

Scurrying around on the hard ground will usually wear down your pet's claws and keep them at a comfortable length. However, if your pet is kept on soft flooring or straw for a long time, the claws may become overgrown and will need trimming by a vet.

Communication

Guinea pigs are very vocal creatures and you will soon come to understand the full range of noises your pet can make and what these might mean. If you startle your guinea pig by trying to pick it up without warning, it is likely to shriek loudly. Generally, guinea pigs make grunting, chattering and squeaking noises, some of which can sound quite odd.

Housing your rabbit and guinea pig

Hutches for rabbits
A hutch for your pet can be bought from a pet shop or you can have one built but in either case, always choose the largest design available. Rabbits like to sit on their haunches and sometimes stand up so a rabbit hutch needs to be tall as well as spacious. It should be at least 60cm (24in) tall and the same width, and a minimum of 91cm (36in) long.

Hutches for guinea pigs
Guinea pigs can live happily in a slightly smaller hutch and a floor area of 60cm (24in) by 45cm (18in) wide is fine for one, but you need to allow an extra 30sq.cm (1sq.ft) for each extra guinea pig. The height of their hutch should be at least 30cm (12in).

● **Above:** *A good hutch offers sufficient shelter, is easy to clean and tall enough to allow a rabbit to stand (opposite).*

Structure

A good hutch will be divided into two parts, each with a separate door with its own secure fastening. One door should be made of mesh on a wooden frame while the other should be completely solid, to provide a retreat for your pet. The hutch should be raised off the ground on sturdy legs and sliding trays in the base make the interior easier to clean out.

Positioning the hutch

Your pet's home must be snug and dry and should be positioned in a sheltered part of the garden where it is not too draughty. A sloped roof covered with roofing felt allows rainwater to run off and keeps out the damp.

Protecting the wood

The outside of a new hutch can be treated with a non-toxic wood preservative but this must be allowed to dry thoroughly before introducing your pet to its new home. The inside should not be treated as your pet may gnaw the wood here.

Exercise areas

It is a good idea to have an outside run or enclosure which allows your pet to exercise and graze on the grass. This can be permanently connected to the hutch so your rabbit and guinea pig can exercise freely, or set up in a separate part of the garden where your pets can be placed for regular periods of time.

● **Right:** *A triangular Morant hutch can be used to house your rabbit or guinea pig during the warm summer months. Your pets will nibble at the grass, so the hutch will need to be moved around the lawn at regular intervals. It is very important to provide a sheltered area which offers protection from the weather.*

Outdoor runs

A suitable run has a wooden framework covered with wire mesh and can be bought from a pet shop or you can have one built specially. The base should be covered with mesh to protect your rabbit or guinea pig from foxes and other predators and to deter burrowing. It is also a good idea to choose a design which enables you to screw the top of the run down for added security.

Providing shelter

Part of the run should be sheltered and clear plastic sheeting can be used to cover one end, part of the sides and the roof above, for this purpose.

Morant hutches

Triangular-shaped runs, sometimes known as Morant hutches, are another alternative, although you should be careful that your pet doesn't escape when you try to catch it as this type of run has a side rather than a roof opening.

Positioning the run

Always position the run in a shady part of the garden and provide a water drinker at all times. It is not unknown for rabbits to die from heat stroke if their run is exposed to direct sunlight during hot weather. The sun will move throughout the day, so check that your pet is safely shaded at all times.

Letting your pet roam free

If you have a secure courtyard, it may be tempting to allow your pet to roam free. Nevertheless, rabbits and especially guinea pigs may be in danger of being attacked by urban foxes or neighbourhood cats.

● **Above:** *You may be tempted to allow your pets to roam free if you have an enclosed garden. Unable to escape, they may be in danger from cats or foxes.*

Keeping your pet indoors

It is becoming increasingly popular to keep these pets, especially rabbits, as household pets indoors. Rabbits can be easily trained to use a cat litter tray and are clean around the home. Unlike cats, they are unlikely to damage furniture, but they may sometimes scratch the carpet.

Making your home safe

When keeping a pet of this type indoors, it is important to keep household plants out of its reach as some can be poisonous if eaten. A rabbit should not be encouraged to climb stairs as a fall could seriously injure its back and may prove fatal. Equally, it is not a good idea to keep a rabbit roaming around the home alongside a dog or cat.

Indoor runs

Guinea pigs should not be allowed to roam free indoors as they tend to disappear under the furniture. You can buy special indoor runs for them similar to an outdoor run. These spacious pens have solid sides and bases which makes them clean to use and a removable mesh cover to keep out curious cats and dogs. The cover can be lifted off to clean the run or feed your pets.

Positioning the run

An indoor run will need to positioned in the shade in a large room and you may find that lack of space makes it unsuitable to keep your pet indoors.

● **Above:** *Rabbits respond well to training and can be taught to use a litter tray.*

Fitting out a hutch

Bedding materials

There are various bedding materials which you can use to line your pet's hutch. Wood shavings are good because they are absorbent and less likely to irritate your pet's eyes than sawdust. These must be bought from a pet shop to be sure they are free of chemicals. Alternatively, you may prefer to choose paper bedding which is cleaner if you are keeping your pet indoors. This is also available from many pet shops.

Hay

Good quality meadow hay must be provided, both as bedding and as food. It can be cheaper to buy a

complete bale rather than small bags, but it must be stored in a dry place. Damp hay will turn mouldy and can make your pet ill. Straw is slightly cheaper than hay, but it is not such a good source of food and the sharp ends of the stalks may injure your pet's eyes.

Food and water containers

Drinking water is best supplied in a drinker bottle which hooks on to the mesh door of the hutch. Bottles with metal spouts are best, as a gnawing pet will soon damage a plastic spout. Fresh and dried foods should be provided in separate dishes. Heavy glazed pottery dishes are best as these are difficult to tip over and easy to clean.

Gnawing material

In addition you should provide a gnawing block for your rabbit or guinea pig to keep its teeth in trim. A log, hard-baked bread or a chew or seed treat bought from a pet shop are good alternatives. If no gnawing material is provided, your pet may start to gnaw at the hutch itself which can be harmful to your pet and cause unnecessary damage.

● *Left: A hutch must be fitted with suitable bedding material, heavy food dishes, a water drinker and hard gnawing material such as a gnawing block.*

33

Cleaning the hutch and run

The hutch and run need regular cleaning to keep your pet healthy and happy. Uneaten food along with any soiled flooring and droppings must be removed every day. The bedding area must also be checked thoroughly to ensure that it is clean and you may need to add extra bedding if the weather is cold.

● *Above:* *The hutch needs to be thoroughly cleaned every week using a stiff brush. The corners need special attention along with the area your pet uses as a toilet.*

Food and water containers
Each day, the food bowls and drinker bottle should be emptied and washed with special animal disinfectant before being re-filled and replaced.

Cleaning out
Once a week, the hutch will need a thorough clean. A stiff brush should be used to sweep out the floor

area and a metal scraper can be used to clean right into the corners. You should clean the area of the hutch that your pet uses as a toilet with a special animal disinfectant.

Maintaining the water drinker

Each week the drinker bottle should be cleaned out with a bottle brush and the spout should be checked for any dirt blocking the opening. Badly cleaned drinker bottles may begin to grow algae which may contaminate the water and upset your pet's stomach.

Long-term care

From time to time, the hutch should be completely stripped out and scrubbed. This is also a good time to make any repairs and to ensure that the hutch is water-proof. Your pet should not be returned to a newly cleaned hutch until it is completely dry.

Maintaining an outdoor run

An outdoor run should be moved at intervals, as the grass becomes short. Avoid leaving it in the same position for long, even if it is not being used as the grass under the sides will die, leaving bare tracks on the lawn.

● **Below:** *An outdoor run should be moved around the lawn to allow the grass to re-grow.*

Questions *and* Answers

Is it worthwhile having a hay rack?
Probably not if you are also providing hay as bedding. Rabbits tend to use just one part of their hutch as a toilet area, leaving areas of clean hay on the floor to eat. However, you should have a hay rack if you decide to keep Peruvian guinea pigs as they must not be kept on hay or straw as it becomes stuck in their long coats, making them difficult to groom.

What is hutch burn?
This usually affects rabbits kept in poor conditions. Inadequate bedding leaves their hind legs and underparts exposed to acidic urine which attacks the hair and skin.
Rex rabbits are most vulnerable because they only have a thin covering of fur on this part of their bodies. An affected rabbit should be treated by a vet to ensure that the exposed areas heal properly and the rabbit's environment should be improved to prevent the problem arising again.

Can I put a run for my guinea pig on our new lawn?
It is best to give the lawn a chance to settle first. Turf is often treated with weed killers or other chemicals which may be harmful and even grass seeds are often coated. An overgrown patch of a vegetable garden is just as suitable as a lawn. Your pets will help to clear the ground and fertilise it with their droppings.

I have a large enclosed garden. Can I let my rabbit roam free?

In a large garden it is often better to section off an area around the hutch as a rabbit enclosure using mesh fencing. This will prevent your pet from eating poisonous plants or encountering other pets such as dogs which may be dangerous. The fence should be at least 1m (3ft) tall and should be sunk into the ground. A secure mesh door should be fitted to allow you access. Leave the hutch door open when the enclosure is in use to allow your pet to shelter from rain or strong sunlight.

● *Above: An outdoor run is perfect for allowing your pet freedom out of their hutch on warm days. Ideally it should be positioned on grass to allow your pet to nibble, but if your lawn is new it is safer to place it on part of an old vegetable garden instead.*

Feeding your pet

Both rabbits and guinea pigs are easy to feed as special pellets and cereal-based food mixtures are widely available from pet shops. However, an ideal diet includes both fresh and dried food and these animals enjoy a wide range of plants, vegetables and even some fruit.

Fresh foods

Some plants such as rhubarb and beetroot leaves are potentially poisonous and are best avoided. The choice of plant foods available largely depends on the time of year. Root vegetables such as carrots are available throughout winter and celery and apple can also be provided.

Preparing fresh foods

All vegetables should be washed thoroughly and peeled if necessary to remove any harmful chemicals and fertilisers.

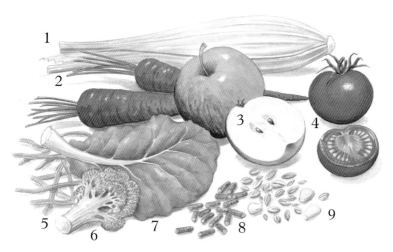

● **Above:** *Suitable foods for a rabbit or guinea pig include: 1. celery 2. carrot 3. apple 4. tomato 5. hay 6. broccoli 7. cabbage 8. rabbit pellets 9. cereals.*

A varied diet

If you introduce a wide range of fresh foods to your pet at an early age, it will continue to enjoy a varied diet as it grows older. Plenty of weeds such as dandelions, chickweed and coltsfoot are suitable as food and some are even believed to act as medicines. A weed called shepherd's purse is thought to help prevent diarrhoea.

Vitamin C

Broccoli and dark green leafy vegetables provide a vital source of Vitamin C for guinea pigs and should be provided regularly. Lighter vegetables such as lettuce have a high water content and are not as nutritious. Guinea pig pellets have added Vitamin C.

CHECKLIST - Suitable foods

For rabbits: Green leafy vegetables, carrot, apple, rabbit pellets, cereals, hay, grass and some weeds

For guinea pigs: Broccoli, dark green leafy vegetables, apple, carrot, celery, tomato, melon, guinea pig pellets, cereals, hay, grass and weeds

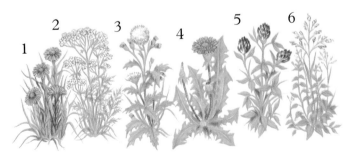

● *Above:* Some weeds are suitable as food for rabbits and guinea pigs. These include: 1. coltsfoot 2. yarrow 3. groundsel 4. dandelion 5. clover 6. chickweed.

39

Grooming and handling

Handling your pet from an early age will do much to win its confidence. Generally, rabbits are easier to catch than guinea pigs, but they can prove to be more of a handful. Never try to pick up a rabbit with bare arms. Rabbits have very strong hind legs and can give a powerful kick, which is likely to cause painful scratches if your arms are not properly protected by long sleeves.

Handling your rabbit

When picking up a rabbit, never support it by its ears alone as this will cause your pet considerable distress. Instead, if you are right-handed, place your left hand in front of the rabbit in its hutch and use the other hand to lift it up from beneath. Once the rabbit is out of the hutch, tuck its hindquarters in between your right arm and the side of your body. In this position, your rabbit should feel quite secure and will be unable to kick.

● **Above:** *Never pick a rabbit up by its ears. The ears may be held to calm the animal, but its weight should be supported by a hand underneath its body.*

● *Above:* When picking up a guinea pig, always use your hand to support it from beneath. Once lifted, never leave the guinea pig's hindquarters unsupported.

Holding it safely

Placing a hand around a rabbit's ears can help to steady it down, if it is struggling badly. You must avoid dropping a rabbit at all costs as even a slight fall can cause a severe back injury. When grooming, always place the rabbit on a level surface such as a table and never leave it unsupervised in case it tries to jump off.

Handling your guinea pig

In the same way as a rabbit, a guinea pig's body should be supported by the right hand, but avoid gripping too tightly as this is likely to prove painful for your pet and could cause internal injuries.

Grooming short-haired varieties

Short-haired rabbits and guinea pigs will groom themselves without help from you, but grooming is still recommended as it will tame your pet and give you a chance to check that its skin and coat are healthy. Grooming once a week with a soft-bristled brush or comb is fine for a short-haired pet.

Long-haired varieties

If you have an Angora rabbit or a long-haired or rough-haired guinea pig, you will need to spend more time and effort grooming its coat to prevent any matts or tangles. Groom it everyday using a stiff-bristled brush, brushing the coat with gentle strokes following the same direction that the fur grows.

● **Above:** *Although short-haired guinea pigs don't really need grooming, it is a good way to tame your pet and allows you to check the condition of its coat and skin.*

Mixing with other pets

Natural predators

Rabbits and guinea pigs should not be allowed to run loose with other pets, particularly dogs or cats. Some breeds of dog have been bred to catch rabbits and will instinctively want to chase your pet. Domesticated rabbits are much tamer and less able to escape from danger than their wild relatives and, what starts out as play, can quickly develop into a deadly encounter. Keep your dog indoors when moving a rabbit or guinea pig in or out of its hutch or run. An excitable dog will distress the rabbit and you may even lose your hold on it causing a fall.

Infectious bites

Most cats will ignore rabbits, although it is not unknown for farm cats to kill smaller varieties. They should therefore be kept apart for safety's sake. Even a minor bite can be dangerous to a guinea pig. Harmful bacteria in a cat's mouth may get into the blood stream through a bite and cause an infection.

● *Above: Rabbits and guinea pigs can usually be kept together with no problems, although you must ensure that the rabbit does not pluck the guinea pig's hair.*

Questions *and* Answers

My pet rabbit doesn't seem to drink much water. Is this normal?
The amount of water taken varies depending on the temperature and the other fluids available. Fresh foods contain a lot of water, so your pet will drink less when given lots of vegetables to eat.

Always make sure that a new rabbit is able to drink from the drinker bottle. Squeeze the bottle of the drinker until water drips out of the spout to attract your pet to it.

During the winter, the water may freeze in the bottle and so you should check every morning that the metal spout isn't blocked with ice and that the water is flowing freely. Do not fill the bottle to the top. The water will expand as it turns to ice and the container may crack.

How often should I feed my rabbit and guinea pig?
Rabbit and guinea pig pellet foods along with fresh hay should be given every day in the morning and again in the evening. Make sure that you fill the water bottle at the same time. Fresh greens should also be given every day and any uneaten fresh food from the previous day should be removed.

Carrots, apples and other vegetables can be given once a day to guinea pigs and every other day to rabbits to keep their diet varied. These should be chopped into small chunks for guinea pigs to make them easier to eat. You will soon get used to how much your pet will eat in one sitting and can supply just the right amount to keep waste to a minimum.

● **Above:** A diet rich in fresh food will provide extra water, but plenty of clean drinking water must still be supplied.

● **Above:** Pellet food is a good source of vitamins and minerals and forms a good basic diet along with fresh foods.

Breeding rabbits and guinea pigs

Breeding animals is a big responsibility and before even considering this you must be sure that you can either keep and care for all the offspring or find good homes for them.

Mating rabbits

Your rabbit will be ready to breed at about five months old in the case of smaller rabbits and slightly older for bigger breeds. When a doe is ready to breed, the skin around her rear end will be reddish rather than the normal pink and she should be moved to the buck's cage. Rabbits have an unusual breeding cycle and the females are able to produce eggs whenever they are placed with males. The mating pair should be left together for several days, after which the doe should be transferred back to her own quarters.

The pregnant doe

A rabbit's pregnancy lasts about 31 days and, towards the end of this period, the doe should be given a box filled with soft hay where she can have her litter. At this stage, she will start to pull out her fur to make a snug nest.

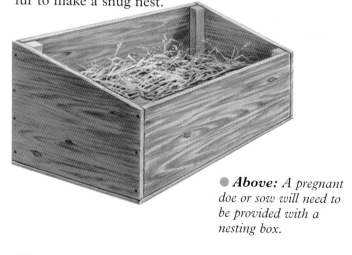

● **Above:** *A pregnant doe or sow will need to be provided with a nesting box.*

● **Above:** *These day-old Dwarf Lop rabbits are kept safe and warm in their nest which has a soft lining made by the mother doe. During her pregnancy, the doe pulls out her fur to make the lining as part of her nesting instinct.*

Mating guinea pigs

It is a good idea to mate guinea pig sows for the first time when they are four or five months old, as they may have difficulty giving birth for the first time at an older age. One or more females can be placed with the male, and they should be left together for several weeks.

The pregnant sow

Pregnancy lasts about 63 days and you should avoid handling her during this period, as it may harm the unborn young.

Caring for the young

Rabbits usually have their young at night and there will be between six and nine kittens in a litter. Does can be nervous mothers, so avoid disturbing the nest or she may desert her offspring or even attack them.

Tending to the young

If there is a problem, you are likely to hear the young rabbits calling repeatedly. If you must inspect the nest, touch the doe first to mask your scent. The doe may be suffering from an infection of her mammary glands called *mastitis*, and in this case you should contact your vet straight away.

The first few weeks

Although naked, blind and helpless at birth, young rabbits grow quickly. Their fur will start to show at four days and five days later their eyes open. They will venture out of the nest when they are just over a fortnight old. The kittens can be parted from their mother at six weeks old when they are feeding themselves. Do not rush this. It is better to wait a few extra days to be sure.

● **Top:** *These day-old rabbits are completely helpless. The nest should not be disturbed for the first few weeks. When the rabbits are feeding themselves at six weeks old (above), they can be parted from their mother.*

Guinea pig litters

Young guinea pigs are born fully developed with a full coat and their eyes open. They are miniatures of their parents at this stage and they will even be nibbling at solid food when just a day or so old. A sow usually gives birth to between one and four youngsters in a litter, but occasionally there may be as many as ten. Guinea pig young are fully independent by about a month old.

A sow should be separated from her mate when she is due to give birth to prevent their breeding again straight away, which can be harmful.

● **Below:** *Although fully developed when born, young guinea pigs should be kept with their mother for at least a month before going to a new home. These are sociable creatures which should be re-housed in small groups.*

Questions *and* Answers

Why does my rabbit pull her coat when she has not been mated?
This can be a sign of a false pregnancy. The doe's body tells her that she is pregnant when she is not, but this phase should pass before long. False pregnancies are most common when two does are kept together.

How can I tell if my doe is pregnant, and when can I mate her again?
A doe may show signs of a false pregnancy within about 17 days of mating. If she is pregnant, she will grow considerably larger after three weeks and it will be clear that she is expecting a litter shortly. Allow about eight weeks after she produced her last litter before mating her again.

My Himalayan guinea pig has lost some of her fur after giving birth. Will it regrow?
This can happen with Red-eyed White guinea pigs in particular, but the effects are only temporary. The hair should regrow within about a month, but consult your vet if the symptoms worsen, as this could indicate an infection.

Does my guinea pig need a special diet when she is pregnant?
She will need extra Vitamin C and so you should feed her regular amounts of green food. Some guinea pigs can become fat if fed only on dry food which can lead to a serious illness called *pregnancy toxaemia*. Loss of appetite and muscular twitching are typical symptoms of this illness and a vet should be consulted immediately in order to save the guinea pig and her babies.

● **Above:** *A pregnant doe pulls its fur to make a soft nest. In a false pregnancy, the rabbit will still follow this instinct.*

● **Above:** *Pregnant guinea pigs need extra Vitamin C in their diet which comes from green, leafy vegetables.*

51

Exhibiting your pet

There is a big difference between the average pet
rabbit or guinea pig and one which is suitable for
showing, but it you do wish to take your pet-keeping
a stage further, there are special shows where you can
exhibit your rabbits and guinea pigs. These are
usually advertised in club journals or specialist
magazines and, if you are interested in this side of
the hobby, then it is best to join a club to keep in
touch with up-and-coming events.

Show-quality animals
It is a good idea to visit some shows before entering
your own animals. The judges will not only look at
the overall condition of your pets, but will award
them points based on what is considered to be the
ideal appearance of the variety concerned. The
desirable features are described in the show standard,
along with characteristics which are considered to be
serious faults. If your rabbit or guinea pig has one of
the faults listed, it will have little chance of winning
and may even be disqualified.

Which breed?

Some breeds are easier to produce to the show standard than others. Generally 'self' coloured varieties are less trouble than those with very precise markings such as the Dutch rabbit which can be difficult to breed to show standard. Pairing two well-marked rabbits is no guarantee that their offspring will be similarly patterned.

Preparing for the exhibition

Preparation and grooming for a show can be time-consuming and hard work. Peruvian guinea pigs need their coats put in special wrappers made of balsa wood and brown paper. The guinea pig will also need to be trained to remain still on a judging stand.

Pet shows

Entering your pet in a major show can be quite expensive and time-consuming. Instead, it may be more suitable to enter your rabbit or guinea pig in a general pet competition. In these events, entries are judged on their character and well-cared-for appearance rather than to a specialist standard.

● **Above:** *Ordinary pets are usually not suitable for exhibiting in shows, but can be entered in general pet competitions where they can win cups and rosettes.*

● **Opposite:** *Show-quality animals are bred to conform to strict ideals and competition is very tough.*

53

Going on holiday

When going away, you must find someone responsible to care for your pets. You may have a friend or neighbour who can look after your rabbit or guinea pig and, in this case, it is best to take your pet in its hutch to their home.

Using a house sitter

If you have a number of pets including dogs and cats, then home sitting may be a good idea. This entails someone coming to stay in your home while the family is away and looking after all the pets. This can work out cheaper than paying to have them kept in a boarding kennels, which is another alternative. Your vet may be able to suggest a reliable home-sitter in your area.

Reciprocal care

If you belong to a local club, you may be able to arrange for another club member to look after your rabbits and guinea pigs when you are on holiday, while you do the same for them when they are away. This is a good idea as you can be sure that they are experienced in caring for these animals.

● **Right:** *When going on holiday you must arrange for someone responsible to look after your pet. With caged animals, it is better to take your pet in its cage to the sitter's house where it will receive round-the-clock care.*

CHECKLIST - *Going on holiday*

- Make arrangements for someone to care for your pet as early as possible.

- Clean out the hutch thoroughly before you go and leave instructions for daily cleaning.

- Supply enough dried food and bedding for the time you are away.

- Make arrangements for the carer to supply fresh foods.

- Write a list of daily care, giving details of how much food to feed and when.

- Leave your vet's name, address and telephone number, along with your pet's name and age in case of emergencies.

The first signs of illness

When properly cared for, rabbits and guinea pigs are healthy animals, but if your pet does become ill, a vet should be consulted straight away. Never attempt to treat an illness yourself and avoid infecting other pets by moving the sick animal to a hutch on its own. The original housing should be thoroughly scrubbed and disinfected.

Upset stomachs

One of the most common health problems is an upset stomach which is usually caused by a sudden change in diet. Allowing your pet to gorge itself on grass in a run after being in a hutch for several days can trigger these symptoms and upset stomachs usually cure themselves.

However, diarrhoea can become, or may be, a sign of an infectious illness. If your rabbit or guinea pig looks unwell or the symptoms persist, contact your vet without delay.

Snuffles

Rabbits can suffer from a disease called *snuffles* which is similar to a cold. An affected rabbit will wipe at its running nose with its paws causing staining, and the eyes may also be affected. This is a difficult illness to treat and sometimes leads to *pneumonia*, which can be fatal.

Ear infections

A rabbit's ears should be checked regularly for signs of ear mites. These cause crusty scabs and an infected rabbit will scratch repeatedly at its itchy ears. This can be treated by dusting the inside of the ears with 'flowers of sulphur'.

Skin mites

Guinea pigs are more likely to suffer from skin mites on their bodies, leading to bald areas. Your vet will be able to supply a special medicated shampoo to treat this condition. As with any infectious illness, the hutch must be scrubbed out thoroughly.

Bites and grazes

Some bald patches and sores are caused by fighting and minor wounds can be bathed with salty water. More serious wounds need to be treated by a vet and, in either case, the incompatible pets need to be re-housed in separate hutches.

● **Above:** *When going to the vet, you need to transport your pet in a suitable carrier designed for pets of this size. A sick animal will already be distressed and the correct carrier will ensure that it is as comfortable as possible.*

CARE CHECKLIST

DAILY

Morning   Provide new dry and fresh foods and re-fill the drinker bottle with fresh water.

Remove any uneaten food from the previous feed and any droppings and soiled bedding.

What to look for   Check that the food has been eaten and the droppings are normal.

Check the water flow through the drinker if the temperature has fallen below freezing overnight.

Afternoon   Top up the dry food and provide extra hay if the weather is likely to be cold.

Place your rabbit or guinea pig in the run along with a water drinker and some dry food.

Evening   Return your pet to its hutch.

What to look for   Close the door carefully. Foxes are most likely to strike at night and can undo loose catches.

WEEKLY

Clean out the hutch, replacing the bedding entirely.

Groom your pet. Some rabbits and guinea pigs with long coats need more frequent grooming.

Wash out the drinker with a bottle brush, cleaning both the bottle and the spout.

Check supplies of food and bedding and buy new supplies as required.

What to look for

Check the hutch for leaks wetting the bedding and repair any holes.

Watch for skin parasites.

Algal growth will turn the sides of the drinker green, particularly in the summer. Some algae can produce harmful poisons.

Store food in a dry place, out of reach of rodents.

MONTHLY

Scrub out the hutch using a safe, non-toxic disinfectant.

What to look for

Do not put your pet back into the hutch until the interior has dried thoroughly.

Check your pet's claws are not overgrown. Overgrown claws curl and grow at an abnormal angle.

Questions *and* Answers

Is myxomatosis still a threat to rabbits?
This untreatable viral illness still affects wild rabbits which can then infect your pet. It is spread directly from rabbit to rabbit, which is one reason for positioning the hutch off the ground. However, mosquitoes and other biting insects can also spread the disease. Swellings on the face and eyes are typical symptoms of *myxomatosis*. Your vet will be able to advise you on how best to safeguard your rabbit from local risks.

What is Viral Haemorrhagic Disease (VHD) of rabbits?
This is a new disease which kills rabbits quickly and often the only sign is a bleeding nose. A special vaccine against *VHD* can be given to protect your pet.

My guinea pig's rear has become swollen, and it appears to be constipated. What should I do?
This condition is called *rectal impaction* and is common in older guinea pigs. Your vet will be able to clear the blockage, but you should also offer plenty of fresh food in the hope of preventing a recurrence.

How should I treat my rabbit or guinea pig if it suffers from a fall?
Take your pet to the vet straight away as it may be suffering from internal injuries or broken limbs. Gently pick it up in the usual way and wrap it in an old towel. Lay it in a strong, secure grocery box punched with air-holes for the journey and try to keep it as calm as possible.

● **Above:** *A sick or injured guinea pig can be taken to the vet in a pet carrier or a strong cardboard box.*

● **Above:** *Rabbits are generally healthy animals, but you should contact a vet at the first sign of illness.*

About my pet

MY PET'S NAME IS
_____

_____

MY PET'S BIRTHDAY IS
_____

Stick a photo of your pet here

WHICH BREED? MY PET IS A
_____

_____

MY PET'S FAVOURITE FOOD IS
_____

_____

MY VET'S NAME IS
_____

_____

MY VET'S TELEPHONE NUMBER IS
_____

_____

Index